HEROES AND WARRIORS

Joshua

CONQUEROR OF CANAAN

MARK HEALY

Plates by RICHARD HOOK

Firebird Books

Also available in this series by the same author:

KING DAVID Warlord of Israel
NEBUCHADNEZZAR Scourge of Zion
JUDAS MACCABEUS Rebel of Israel

For my Father

Acknowledgements

Many of the quotations herein are taken from *The New Jerusalem Bible* published by Darton Longman & Todd, whose translation and permission is gratefully acknowledged. For information on the military forces, the work of the Wargames Research Group is acknowledged and recommended.

First published in the UK 1989 by Firebird Books
P.O. Box 327, Poole, Dorset BH15 2RG

Copyright © 1989 Firebird Books Ltd
Text copyright © 1989 Mark Healy

Distributed in the United States by
Sterling Publishing Co, Inc
Two Park Avenue, New York, NY 10016

Distributed in Australia by
Capricorn Link (Australia) Pty Ltd
P.O. Box 665, Lane Cove, NSW 2066

British Library Cataloguing in Publication Data

Healy, Mark
  Joshua: conqueror of Canaan
  1. Bible. O.T. Joshua. Characters: Joshua
  I. Title II. Hook, Richard III. Series
  222'.20924

ISBN 1 85314 010 4

Series editor Stuart Booth
Designed by Kathryn S.A. Booth
Typeset by Inforum Typesetting, Portsmouth
Monochrome origination by Castle Graphics, Frome
Colour separation by Kingfisher Facsimile
Colour printed by Barwell Colour Print Ltd (Midsomer Norton)
Printed and bound in Great Britain at The Bath Press

Joshua

CONQUEROR OF CANAAN

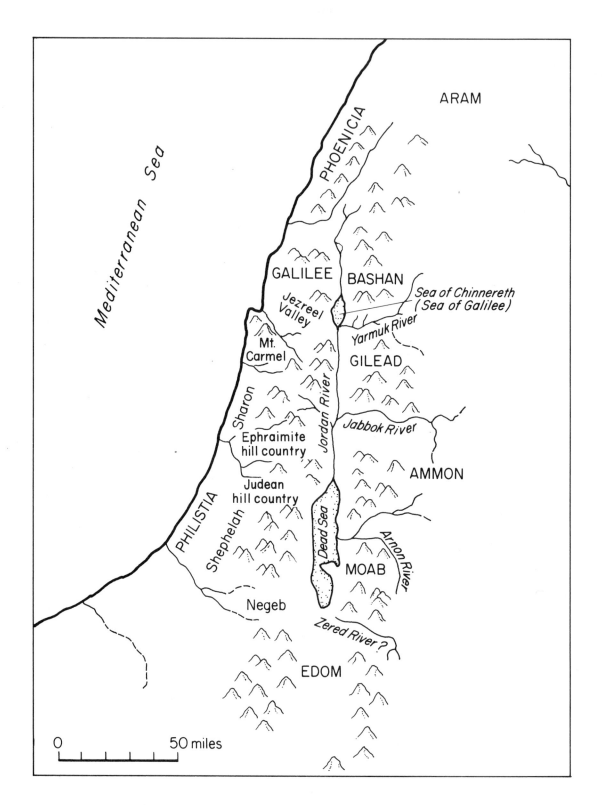

Mediterranean Sea

ARAM

PHOENICIA

GALILEE BASHAN

Jezreel
Valley

Sea of Chinnereth
(Sea of Galilee)

Yarmuk River

Mt.
Carmel

GILEAD

Sharon

Jordan River

Jabbok River

Ephraimite
hill country

AMMON

Judean
hill country

PHILISTIA

Dead Sea

Shephelah

Arnon River

MOAB

Negeb

Zered River?

EDOM

0   50 miles

4

Joshua captured the entire country, just as Yahweh had told Moses, and he gave it as heritage to Israel to be shared out between the tribes.

(Joshua 11:23)

Warrior Son of Nun

On the face of it, the Bible tells a straightforward enough story of Joshua, the great Hebrew warrior and successor to Moses. He emerges in the *Book of Exodus* as the 'adjutant of Moses'; the first evidence we are given of his military prowess is when he is appointed by Moses to command an attack on the nomadic Amalekites, who were harrying the Israelites in what was probably a series of guerrilla attacks. Already the efficient commander, Joshua, 'defeated Amalek, putting their people to the sword' (*Exodus* 17:13).

Joshua continued in this subordinate role until Moses' death, when he took over the leadership of the Israelites. Moses had, not long before his death, nominated him as his successor:

Joshua, son of Nun, was filled with the spirit of wisdom, for Moses had laid his hands on him . . .

(Deuteronomy 34:9)

Under Joshua's command, the Israelites crossed the River Jordan and occupied Canaan, their Promised Land. Then he led them in the wars that followed their occupation of the land.

Moses had died without setting foot on the ground of the Promised Land towards which he had led his people; but he had welded the Israelites together during the long years in the wilderness and in a sense his work was done. What was needed at his death was not another charismatic prophet, not a second maker of a nation, but a practical soldier, a warrior. This was the part that Joshua played.

It seems to hang together well enough. But the man behind this story remains a curious and challenging mystery. Some scholars have doubted his very existence.

The problem lies in the sources upon which we have to rely. There is little or no corroborative evidence to be found in history or archaeology for the story as told in the *Book of Joshua* – and the purpose of that book was neither historical nor biographical but, primarily, religious. For its compiler, the most important purpose of the text was to show that it was through the action of God, not man, that Canaan was delivered into the

The likely appearance of the Amalekites and other tribes against whom first Joshua and later Gideon fought.

Dating from the Egyptian late Middle Kingdom, this tomb painting from Beni-hasen captures well the colourful garb – the 'coats of many colours' – of a group of Semitic nomads who came down to Egypt to trade.

hands of the Israelites. After all, they were the chosen people of their god – Yahweh. Consequently, the concern of the compilers of the *Book of Joshua* was to describe the events through which God fulfilled his promise to give the Israelites a land of their own. This, naturally, means that Joshua has to be given a subsidiary rôle.

Joshua emerges as a leader who operates under the direction of Yahweh, upon whose word his actions are almost entirely dependent. On the one occasion, when he does not consult his God, but acts of his own accord by sending spies to assess the defences of the city of Ai, the enterprise ends in failure. So we never gain any insight into Joshua as an individual, because we are given none of the biographical information that might allow us to flesh him out as a person. It is only as the servant of Yahweh that he is presented, even at his death:

. . . Joshua, the son of Nun, servant of Yahweh, died; he was a hundred and ten years old. He was buried on the estate he received as his heritage, at Mount Timnath-Serah which lies in the highlands of Ephraim, north of Mount Gaash.

(*Joshua* 24:29–30)

Another problem is that the *Book of Joshua* was compiled hundreds of years later than the events it described, and was put together by editors who came from the southern kingdom of Judah. However, Joshua was a hero-figure in the traditions of the tribes of central Canaan, the forebears of the northern kingdom of Israel. The southern compilers probably deliberately 'edited out' Joshua because of the antipathy that had long existed between the tribes that formed the two kingdoms. Neither kingdom existed at the time of Joshua – both emerged from the much later political convulsion that split the united kingdom of Israel during the reign of Reheboam, successor of Solomon. So retrospective editing, the rewriting of history, has obscured our knowledge even more.

That being so, we have to approach Joshua in a rather roundabout way – to sneak up on him. We have to place his story, and those of the Judges,

Mediterranean Sea

ASHER

NAPHTALI

DAN(2)

Sea of Galilee

Bashan

ZEBULUN

ISSACHAR

M A N A S S E H

EPHRAIM

DAN (1)

GAD

Jordan

Ammon

BENJAMIN

Jerusalem

(R E U B E N)

J U D A H

Dead Sea

(S I M E O N)

Moab

Negeb

Edom

in a broader context. The conquest of Canaan must be seen as part of a much wider picture, embracing Canaan and its long relationship with Egypt. Furthermore, the story of the sojourn of the tribes in Egypt has to be set against Egypt's relations with infiltrating immigrants such as the 'Asiatics' and, in particular, the Hyksos. It was their substantial legacy

Division of the 'Promised Land' in territories awarded by Joshua to the twelve tribes. An idealised picture rather than one corresponding to actual events of the late twelfth century B.C.

that provided the impetus for Egypt's imperial drive in the New Kingdom period, creating a wider view of the world and utilising a military technology whose impact was to change fundamentally the basis of Egyptian power. Consequently, the introduction of the war chariot was to have a profound effect on the ability of the Israelites to deal with the warlords of the Canaan plains. It was the decline of Egyptian power in Canaan that created the conditions that allowed the Israelites to enter Canaan as intruders and successfully impose themselves on the land and in time take it for themselves.

This period is a rich tapestry of military, political and religious elements. All of them interact to form the immense backdrop to the conquest of the Land of Canaan by the Israelites.

Egypt and Exodus

Because, as we have seen, Joshua enters upon the stage of history as a military commander appointed by Moses, he is in a very real sense a child of the Exodus. He is a product of the most pivotal event in the long history of the Jewish people, when the Hebrews escaped from their bondage in Egypt and set out on their journey to the Promised Land. The story is recalled annually today by Jews the world over when, at the celebration of the Passover, the head of the household reads aloud the story of the Exodus.

The Despised Asiatic

The Exodus itself had its roots deep in the Hebrews' past, for they had been resident in the kingdom of Egypt for hundreds of years. They were among a number of tribes – known collectively to the Egyptians as 'Asiatics' – who from time immemorial had infiltrated Egypt from beyond its eastern borders, in particular from Canaan and Syria. The Egyptians looked upon them with contempt mixed with fear, 'the wretched Asiatic', strange peoples with strange ways. A document from the Tenth Dynasty (2134–2040 B.C.) says:

bad is the country where he lives, inconvenient in respect of water, impracticable because of many trees, its roads are bad on account of the mountains. He does not settle in one place, for [lack of] food makes his legs take flight. Since the day of Horus he has been at war, he does not conquer, nor yet can he be conquered.

Not surprisingly, the Asiatics found Egypt preferable to their own homelands and brought their flocks to graze in the Nile delta.

To Egyptian eyes, there would have been nothing to distinguish the Hebrews from any other Asiatics. They had come to escape famine in their own territories in Canaan and they settled – with their cattle, their sheep and all their other possessions – in the land of Goshen, the eastern district of the Nile delta.

This Semitic nomad warrior, again based upon Beni-hasen painting, shows the duck-billed axe, double convex bow and quiver that were the standard weapons around 1900 B.C. and with which Joshua's men would have been armed.

The Hyksos

Egypt tolerated these nomad tribes because they brought some economic benefit to the country, but they were always difficult to contain. In the end, one more powerful and better-organised group, the *Hikau Khasut* or *Hyksos*, effectively took control of Egypt. Exploiting Egyptian political weakness, itself a consequence of a complex of factors, the Hyksos were firmly ensconced in the eastern delta as early as 1720 B.C. and were sufficiently strong to capture the old Egyptian capital city of Memphis in 1674 B.C. After that, Egypt was ruled by foreign (Hyksos) kings, for although the Hyksos rulers physically occupied only Lower Egypt, their power and influence was such that the rest of the country was reduced to a state of virtual vassaldom.

These Hyksos pharaohs, Egypt's Sixteenth Dynasty, so far from imposing an alien culture on Egypt adopted and borrowed extensively from the civilisation over which they ruled. Their names were written in hieroglyphs, they adopted Egyptian throne names and, in the manner of the Pharaohs, they instituted an official religion modelled on that of Egypt. They were so like the native rulers in maintaining a continuity with Egyptian culture and tradition that many in Egypt acquiesced quite contentedly with their rule.

House of Joseph

They retained, too, an essentially Egyptian bureaucracy, but they permitted other 'foreigners' to rise to positions of considerable power within it. The story of Joseph is thus credible in principle, even though it is presented in the Bible in a way whose detail suggests that much of it is fictitious and even though, again, it is recounted for theological rather than historical purposes. Joseph, the favourite of the many sons of the Hebrew patriarch Jacob, rose from being a household slave in Egypt to

Peaceful trade was tempered by the Egyptian policy of punitive campaigns in the Sinai and Canaan – and so the image of the Pharaoh 'smiting the Asiatic' became a recurring motif in Egyptian art.

9

become governor, or vizier, of the whole of Egypt. He took an Egyptian wife, by whom he had two sons, Manasseh and Ephraim, whose descendants became known as the House of Joseph.

At a time of widespread famine his father Jacob, in Canaan, sent his brothers to Egypt to buy grain. Joseph provided them with grain, and revealed his identity to them. Then he asked them to bring Jacob to be re-united with him in Egypt. So Jacob came to live 'in the best of the land; in the land of Goshen' and he and his descendants and all the Hebrews lived peaceably enough under the apparently tolerant rule of the Pharaohs.

We cannot with any confidence ascribe a date to the Joseph story. It would fit in with what we know of Egyptian history at any time from about 2000 B.C. to 900 B.C. The events described, though, drop most neatly into the Hyksos period – at no time afterwards did any Asiatics hold as much sway in Egypt. A career like Joseph's would have been far less credible at any other time.

Probably, however, the only near-certainty that emerges from this whole Joseph story is that a number of tribes from Canaan migrated to Egypt as a consequence of famine and that they remained in Egypt for a very long period of time.

Slavery

The Hyksos were finally expelled from Egyptian soil by Amosis I, the first pharoah of the Eighteenth Dynasty. In a series of campaigns, Memphis was captured and the Hyksos capital, Avaris, in the delta, was sacked. With the tolerant Hyksos rulers gone, in about 1550 B.C., it is possible that life was not so easy for the descendants of Joseph in Egypt. Under the rulers of the Nineteenth Dynasty conditions worsened still more.

The substantial change in the Hebrews' circumstances, from those revealed in the Joseph narrative at the end of *Genesis* to the desperate state described at the beginning of *Exodus*, is explained in the Bible by the simple statement that 'There came to power in Egypt a new king who had never heard of Joseph', who introduced taskmasters over the Israelites to wear them down by forced labour.

Biblical scholars now tend to agree that the Pharoah identified here – the pharaoh of the Exodus – was Ramesses II, who ruled Egypt for the greater part of the thirteenth century B.C. Soon after his accession, he embarked upon the building of a new, fortified residence city, bearing his name, together with a smaller satellite 'store' city, Pithom, both in the eastern delta. This was the land in which the Hebrew tribes grazed their flocks. A vast labour force was needed to build these new cities and for the unskilled tasks – the heavy labouring, the brick making and the mortar mixing – the Hebrews were a convenient pool of manpower. The bondage they endured as forced labourers was harsh.

Even from an early period, it seems that the skills of the Semitic musicians were highly prized by the Egyptians, in whose employ they readily found work.

The Great Escape

How, led by Moses, the Hebrews fled from their slavery in Egypt into the desert of Sinai is told in the *Book of Exodus*, in what must be the greatest escape story of all time. Yet we have few hard facts to go on. The historical evidence is scanty, and the Bible story regards the Exodus as a divine deliverance rather than an epic.

It is generally accepted that the Exodus from Egypt took place during the long reign of Pharaoh Ramesses II. He is depicted here in the famous granite statue from Elephantine.

If we accept that the reference to Israel on the Merneptah Stela is to the House of Joseph that came out of Egypt under the leadership of Moses then it would be reasonable to date the Exodus around 1270–1260 B.C. However, such a date presupposes that the Hebrews really did spend 'forty years' in the wilderness, which may be doubtful given the significance of the figure forty to the Biblical writers. It is entirely possible that the wanderings in the Sinai occupied a much shorter space of time.

Of one matter, however, there seems to be little doubt. The number given in the Bible of the people who came out of Egypt is plainly exaggerated or in error:

The Israelites left Ramesses for Succoth, about six hundred thousand on the march – men, that is, not counting their families.

(*Exodus* 12:37)

This would mean a total of some two and a half million people – a figure that would give a column some 150 miles long of people marching ten abreast. It seems much more reasonable to accept the view that this passage from *Exodus* is quite late and that the figures represent the entire population of Israel at some later time.

It is not at all certain that all those who left Egypt travelled to Canaan as one group. There are a number of traditions preserved which imply that they did not. It seems, too, that, so far from 'all Israel' being involved in the sojourn and subsequent servitude in Egypt, only those related to the House of Joseph – that is the descendants of Manasseh and Ephraim – were involved. Many of the other tribes that came to form the later tribal

The Book of Exodus *tells of bricks made by the Israelites. They would have been of a type very similar to this one, bearing the royal stamp of Ramesses II.*

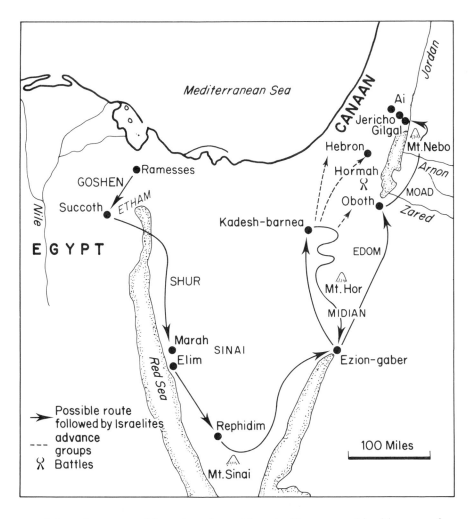

Traditional route of the Exodus from Egypt.

confederation were either already resident in Canaan and had been so for many hundreds of years, or they were not related to the Hebrews at all, being Canaanites who joined with the invaders under Joshua and entered into the covenant that ultimately bound the Hebrews together at a later date, possibly at Shechem.

We do not even know the route of the Exodus – indeed it is more likely that there was no single route, but that a number of different Hebrew groups left Egypt by different routes and made their own different ways across the Sinai peninsula.

Hyksos Military Legacy

The Hyksos bequeathed to the Egyptians much that was to be of great benefit. Under the Hyksos Pharaohs, Egypt became open to new

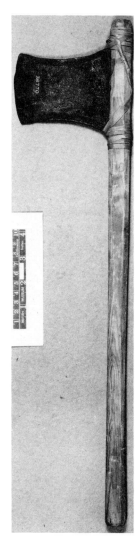

influences from Canaan and Mesopotamia and to new ideas in religion, art and philosophy. But it is in the military innovations that occurred in Egypt because of the Hyksos domination that we can see the greatest immediate impact. Out of the bitter lessons of nearly a century of warfare with the Hyksos, the Pharaohs of Egypt created a powerful and highly effective army with which they were to forge for Egypt an empire in Canaan and beyond.

The Hyksos were able to gain an initial foothold in Egypt because they effectively exploited the country's political weakness. But they gained and maintained their dominance because their military technology was more sophisticated than that of the Egyptians. The Hyksos had the chariot, the compound bow and bronze weaponry and these gave them an overwhelming superiority in battle. When finally, the native Theban pharaohs of the Eighteenth Dynasty were able to overthrow Hyksos power it was largely because they had by now acquired these weapons and learned to use them in a highly effective manner.

It is these weapons and tactics that were to dominate warfare in Egypt and beyond – and, especially, Canaan – for the next five hundred years.

The Chariot

The first chariots probably appeared in Mesopotamia, at least a thousand years before the Hyksos introduced them into Egypt. They had two or four solid wheels and were pulled by asses. The much more mobile spoke-wheeled chariot seems to have been introduced early in the second millennium B.C. in an area where the horse was known and already domesticated, perhaps northern Syria or northern Mesopotamia.

The chariot in the Bronze Age demonstrated a number of improvements. The axle moved further back to the rear of the cab, to provide a more stable firing platform for the archer and driver, although in Egypt it was not until the end of the fifteenth century B.C. that the axle was

By the reign of Tutankhamun, war chariots had acquired distinctively Egyptian features, such as the axle at the rear of the cab and six-spoked wheel and the holder for the compound bow.

moved so far back as to be flush with the rear of the body. Egyptian chariots and their crews acquired armour. This has been illustrated on the walls of tombs – there is a painting of a bronze coat of mail from the tomb of one Kenamon, the steward of Amenophis II, and some relics of bronze scales were found in the palace of Amenophis III in Thebes.

That the chariot had been introduced into Egypt by the Hyksos was acknowledged whenever in Egypt they were spoken of – the terms for the parts of the chariot were all borrowed from the Canaanite. Canaanites were used, too, both to drive and to maintain the chariots. Until the fourteenth century B.C. Egyptian chariots could not readily be distinguished from those used by the Canaanites, but during the reign of Tuthmosis IV the chariots begin to acquire a definite 'Egyptian' identity. Because they had became much heavier they were fitted with an eight-spoke wheel, although wartime experience saw the builders finally settle for six spokes. The chariot taken from the tomb of the young Tutankhamun, which dates from the second half of the fourteenth century, has a cab just over three feet wide and the width of the whole vehicle from wheel to wheel along the axle rod is nearly six feet. This, combined with a height of only four feet and a body width of just four-sevenths the length of the rod, suggests a vehicle both easy to control and, with a well-trained driver and horse team, highly manoeuverable – a vehicle at once agile and stable as a firing platform.

Horses

The Egyptians used two-man chariots. In this they had little choice, for

For rapid transit, a rudimentary chariot design with open cab sides was employed, as is shown in this wall painting.

15

they did not have horses large enough to pull heavier three-man chariots. The horses brought to Egypt by the Hyksos, and subsequently used by the Egyptians, would be described today as ponies, as is shown by an example found buried with full honours near the tomb of Senenmut, the chief steward of Queen Hatshepsut (1473–1458 B.C.). It is a small mare, standing not more than 12½ hands high.

It took some time for Egypt to become a horse-rearing country – climate and geography have not endowed the land with extensive acres of rolling grassland suitable for the grazing of large numbers of horses and horses were in short supply. Because of this, while the army of Amosis that finally ejected the Hyksos from Egypt did possess and use chariots we have to presume that the Egyptian chariot arm was at that time quite small, although no doubt swollen by captured Hyksos chariots. It remained relatively small until at least the time of Tuthmosis III. The maintenance of a chariot arm was always for this reason, a burden upon the state's resources. It became a major objective of its use in war to help acquire in the booty taken from the enemy other horses and chariots that could then be employed in the Egyptian ranks and used to swell the breeding stock in Egypt itself. Following the Battle of Megiddo, in 1458 B.C., some 2041 horses as well as 191 foals, some stallions and a number of colts were specifically picked out in the description of the booty taken from the defeated forces of the Canaanite alliance, some small indication of their importance to the Egyptians.

The Compound Bow
Although Egyptian soldiers of the Old and Middle Kingdoms had long employed the stave bow as their principal long-range weapon, it was through the Hyksos that they first encountered the much more formidable compound bow. The principal advantages of the compound bow lay in its greater range combined with a remarkable penetrative power. It is little wonder therefore that in many armies it became one of the standard weapons of war allowing combat to begin at quite long ranges. However, there is always a price to be paid for technological advance; in the case of the compound bow it was in the complexity of its manufacture. Additionally, its cost of production, arising principally out of the materials employed in its manufacture, meant it was not used by all the troops equipped as archers. Thus, in the Egyptian army of the New Kingdom it was common to find the stave bow employed alongside the compound bow, with the latter weapon being mainly restricted to the chariotry, who needed its penetrative power to deal with the armourclad crews of Egypt's enemies.

Some insight into the materials needed for production of the compound bow can be gauged from *The Tale of Aqhat*, an epic found on a number of tablets excavated at the site of ancient Ugarit in northern Syria, destroyed by the Sea Peoples in the twelfth century:

The Book of Joshua tells how Jericho succumbed to Israelite attack. On the seventh day of marching around the city, its walls collapsed. It was totally destroyed, together with its inhabitants.

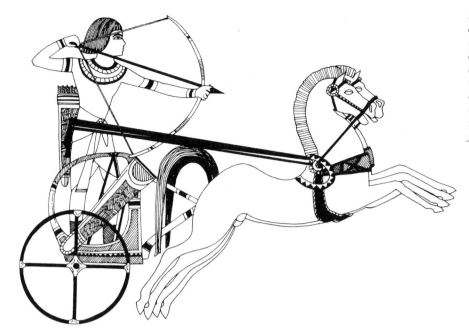

I vow yew trees of Lebanon,
I vow sinews from wild oxen;
I vow horns from mountain goats,
Tendons from the hocks of a bull;
I vow from arcane forest reeds:
Give [these] to Kothar wa-Khasis.
He'll make a bow for thee,
Darts for Yabamat-Liimmim

Thus, the process of creating a compound bow required materials from at least three animals and one tree. The arrows were made from reeds and fitted with bronze arrowheads (darts) which were necessary if the scale armour worn by the chariot crews of the enemy was to be penetrated. Thus, the equipping of an archer with a compound bow was a complex and expensive business.

The bows illustrated in Egyptian sources are either triangular or the recurved type. The materials from which they were constructed were very susceptible to warping due to changes in climatic conditions. Consequently, these bows were placed in their own cases when not in use and such cases can be observed on the sides of chariots. Some sense of the power of this weapon in the hands of an expert skilled in its use can be gauged from an account of the training of Pharaoh Amenophis II. He practised with the weapon from a chariot being driven at the gallop;

He [the king] entered into the northern garden and found that there had been set up for him four targets of Asiatic copper of one palm in their thickness, with twenty cubits between one post and its fellow . . . In his chariot, he grasped his bow and gripped four arrows at the same time . . . shooting at [the targets]. His arrows come out of the back

Caught in the mud, the 'iron' chariots of Sisera and the Canaanites succumbed to the attack of the Israelites swarming down from Mount Tabor under the command of Barak and Deborah.

thereof while he was attacking another post. It really was a deed which had never been done nor heard of by report: shooting at a target or copper an arrow which came out of it and dropped to the ground . . .

While other weapons made a significant contribution to warfare in the Bronze Age it was the chariot and the composite bow that were by far the dominating features of the battlefield. Their use released a level of mobility and destruction hitherto not seen in warfare. The Israelites, as we shall see, found the Canaanites of the cities of the plains formidable opponents because they were able to deploy weapons as destructive as these.

Conquest of Canaan

The most popular picture of the Israelite tribes coming into the inheritance promised to them by Yahweh is the Biblical account of the conquest of Canaan by the twelve tribes under the unified command of Joshua. The *Book of Joshua* gives a dramatic account of 'All Israel' participating in three campaigns in the middle, south and north of the country that see the destruction of many of the leading Canaanite cities and the subjugation of the people under Israelite rule.

The Promised Land

Nowadays, the name of Canaan is rarely encountered outside the pages of the Bible. Nevertheless, it was a term familiar not only to Joshua – and the people he led as the object of their predatory design – but also to many other ancient peoples. Evidence exists for the employment of the term in cuneiform, the diplomatic *lingua franca* of the ancient Near East. In that form, it occurs in texts from Syria, Phoenicia and Egypt. In the later period, the name was sufficiently understood by the Greeks and the Romans for them to employ it in historical writings. The geographical area to which the name refers is variously defined, but always centred on those lands identified with the more familiar (but much later) name of Palestine.

The origin of the name is still a matter of some dispute, although it is generally regarded as deriving from an Akkadian word *kinakhkhu*, meaning 'reddish purple'. As such, it would seem to have arisen from an identification of the land with the purple dye industry in ancient Phoenicia, which corresponds to the contemporary country of the Lebanon in addition to lands which now form part of Israel and Syria.

The first known use of the name is found on a magnesite statue of one Idri-mi of Alalakh, a city of some importance in the second millenium B.C. built astride one of the route junctions connecting northern Syria,

Bronze dagger from the thirteenth–fourteenth centuries B.C. Such a fine weapon would once have adorned the waistband of a high ranking soldier in the Pharaoh's army and inspired designs among the weapons of their enemies.

Mesopotamia and the Hittite kingdom in Anatolia. The statue dates from around 1550 B.C. when Idri-mi was ruler of Alalakh and a vassal of Parattarna, King of Mitanni. Idri-mi wrote his autobiography in a hundred and four lines of cuneiform inscribed all over the figure. He tells how he left his family in Emar:

I took with me my horse, my chariot and my groom, went away and crossed over the desert country and even entered into the region of the Sutian warriors. I stayed with them [once] over night in my . . . chariot, but the next day I moved on and went to the land of Canaan. I stayed in Ammia in the land of Canaan; in Ammia lived also natives of Haleb, of the country of Mukishkhi, of the country Ni' and also warriors from the country Ama'e. They discovered that I was the son of their overlord and gathered around me.

Idri-mi of Alalakh, on whose statue inscribed in cuneiform is the first known reference to the Land of Canaan.

There I grew up and stayed a long time. For seven years I lived among the Hapiru people.

Plainly the land of Canaan spoken of by Idri-mi lay to the south of his homeland and it would seem that the Egyptians understood Canaan to encompass the lands of modern Lebanon and Israel starting in the south at Gaza and stretching eastwards to the River Jordan and the Bekaa valley. Thus they applied it to a fairly limited geographical area, giving the name Retenu to the Sinai, Canaan and Syria combined.

Of all the Biblical allusions to the extent of Canaan one of the most detailed is that given in *Numbers 34* where the land as defined by Yahweh, the god of Israel, is more or less identical in its extent with the Egyptian province of Canaan at the end of the thirteenth century B.C. It seems that it was from Egyptian usage that the Israelites took over the term for the land that for nearly three thousand years has been bound to the history and destiny of the Jewish people.

Who were the inhabitants of Canaan at the time when Joshua led his troops into the land? We have already met the Hapiru, with whom

Dated from the same period as the el-Amarna tablet is this depiction of the captive Canaanite in chains.

One of many cuneiform tablets discovered at el-Amarna and dating from the fourteenth century B.C. in which Yapahu, the ruler of Gezer, corresponded with the Egyptian court as to conditions in Canaan. Mentioned in the letter are Hapiru, who are possibly identified with the Hebrews.

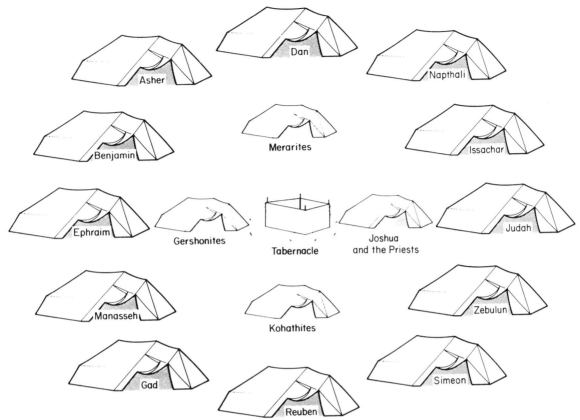

Asher · Dan · Napthali · Benjamin · Merarites · Issachar · Ephraim · Gershonites · Tabernacle · Joshua and the Priests · Judah · Manasseh · Kohathites · Zebulun · Gad · Reuben · Simeon

Idri-mi stayed. These seem to have been stateless freebooters who sold their services as mercenaries and, doubtless, as lawless bands, exploited any breakdown in the authority of the Egyptian overlords. The population was certainly a heterogeneous one. But mostly Canaan was comprised of small city states with a feudal social structure supporting an aristocracy of charioteers, known as the maryannu. Vassal responsibility meant that the king of each city state would in time of war call his maryannu to arms in the service of the pharaoh.

Invasion

Joshua entered Canaan, according to the Biblical text, at the head of some 40,000 warriors (*Joshua* 3:13) although at the battle of Ai he deploys only some 5000 (*Joshua* 8:12), which seems a more credible figure.

No information is given about the arms and equipment of the Israelite forces, but almost certainly their principal weapons were the same as those of other nomadic intruders into Canaan – the sword, spear and bow. Tomb paintings in Egypt show clearly that nomadic Asiatics were metalworkers and so it seems perfectly reasonable to assume that the Israelites were well able to make their own weapons. The main weapon would have probably been the bronze khopesh sword and the major

Like all desert tribes, the Israelites would have set up their camp with each tribe as a fighting unit in its specific position. But their encircled tents also protected the Tabernacle containing the Ark, which enshrined their covenant with Yahweh. This inclusion of all the tribes is in keeping with the Biblical description of 'all Israel' as the invading force entering Canaan.

The warring peoples of the invasion period were well able to make their own weapons. The ability of nomads to work metal in this way is well attested here, where asses are shown carrying an anvil and ingots of copper – although by the time of the invasion of Canaan itself, weapons were manufactured mainly in bronze.

long-range weapon the compound bow, whose method of construction was by this time widely known and whose assembly a task easily undertaken by nomads.

From Gilgal the tribes struck inland from the Jordan where some six miles north of the Dead Sea they came upon the city of Jericho.

The Battle of Jericho

Joshua marched the Israelites to within sight of the city walls at which the inhabitants, whom we know already from earlier on in the *Book of Joshua* to be panic-stricken at the coming of the intruders, shut the gates of the city.

Then, acting on Yahweh's instructions, for seven days, bearing the ark before them, the Israelites marched around the walls in silence, apart from trumpets sounded by the priests preceding the ark. On the seventh day, having marched around the city seven times, at Joshua's word of command:

The people raised the war cry, the trumpets sounded. When the people heard the sound of the trumpet, they raised a mighty war cry and the wall collapsed then and there. At once the people stormed the city, each man going straight forward; and they captured the city. They enforced the curse of destruction on everyone in the city: men and women, young and old, including the oxen, the sheep and the donkeys slaughtering all.

(*Joshua* 6:20–21)

But great difficulties are raised when this account is matched against archaeological evidence from extensive excavations carried out at the site. These suggest that at the time of Joshua's invasion Jericho was already a ruin; it had been destroyed in about 1560 B.C. While there is evidence to suggest that there may have been a small settlement at Jericho between 1400 and 1325 B.C., there is none to confirm that Jericho was a major city site in the time of Joshua. They are parallels elsewhere, though, for the stratagem that the Israelites are said to have employed at

Jericho. In a work on military ruses, the Roman writer Frontius reported:

When Domitius Calvinus was besieging Lueria, a town of the Ligurians protected not only by its location and siegeworks but also by the superiority of its defenders he instituted the practice of marching frequently around the walls with all his forces, and then marching back to camp. When the townspeople had been induced to believe that the Roman commander did this for the purpose of drill, and consequently took no precautions against his efforts, he transformed this practice of parading into a sudden attack, and gaining possession of the walls, forced the inhabitants to surrender.

(Yigal Yadin *The Art of Warfare in Biblical Lands*)

Destruction of Ai

Another military ruse was employed by Joshua in effecting the capture and destruction of the city of Ai. At dawn Joshua showed himself and a small force of five thousand men on the plain in front of the city. Thinking that they had an overwhelming superiority of numbers, the king and his forces came out of the city to give battle. Joshua pretended to retreat before them and so drew them away from the city. But the bulk of the Israelite force was concealed on the other side of the city, and this force occupied Ai and put it to fire. Seeing the smoke from the burning city, the people of Ai wavered and began to withdraw. Turning, Joshua and his men chased them back to the city, where the main Israelite force had deployed to act as an anvil to Joshua's hammer:

Although extensively excavated there is no archaeological evidence to support the otherwise widely renowned account of the destruction of Jericho described in the Book of Joshua. Nevertheless, it remains an intriguing and inspiring story of religiously inspired military achievement.

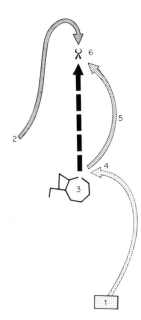

Joshua did not draw back the hand with which he had pointed the sabre until he had subjected all the inhabitants of Ai to the curse of Destruction.

(Joshua 8:26)

Once again, though, the biblical story is at variance with archaeological evidence. Excavations at Ai reveal that the site had long been a ruin when Joshua arrived at Canaan, having been devastated as early as 2000 B.C.

Southern Campaign

In the wake of the destruction of Ai, the inhabitants of Gibeon near Jerusalem entered into a treaty with the Israelites. This is explained away in the Bible as being a consequence of Gibeonite underhandedness, but it shows that the Israelite invaders were prepared to come to an accommodation with the natives where necessary. As a consequence, the King of Jerusalem, Adoni-Zedek, forged an alliance between himself and four other Canaanite kings, those of Hebron, Jarmuth, Lachish and Eglon. Combining their forces they advanced on Gibeon and placed it under siege. The Gibeonites sent word of their predicament to Joshua, who marched through the night and attacked the Canaanite forces at first light, pursuing the fleeing enemy down the defile at Beth-Horon. (Over a thousand years later Judas Maccabeus was to catch his enemies in the pass at Beth-Horon in a like manner.) The forces of the five kings were routed. The five kings were discovered hiding in a cave and taken to Joshua, who killed them and had their bodies thrown into a cave.

Joshua and the Israelites then moved south and conquered the cities of southern Canaan. It was a campaign of great destructiveness as the Bible makes plain:

Thus Joshua subjugated the whole country: the high lands, the Hegeb, the lowlands and watered foothills, and all their kings. He left not one survivor and put every living thing under the curse of destruction, as Yahweh, God of Israel, had commanded. Joshua conquered them as far as Kadesh-Barnea to Gaza and the whole region of Goshen as far as Gibeon. All these kings and their territory Joshua captured in a single campaign, because Yahweh, God of Israel fought for Israel.

(Joshua 10:40–42)

Again, though, we are in difficulties with the evidence. The cities described as being conquered by Joshua in this southern campaign were for the most part conquered by the Israelites only at a much later date. Jerusalem remained firmly in the hands of the Jebusites until it was taken by David some two centuries later. Indeed, we find in the *Book of Judges* (1:21) that the tribe of Benjamin who came to inhabit the area were unable to eject them from the city. Gezer is also said to have been taken by Joshua, but is known not to have been taken by the Israelites until the reign of Solomon. There would seem, in fact, to be no real evidence to support the picture given in the Bible of a southern campaign by Joshua and 'All Israel'.

The Battle of Ai. 1: Joshua's large force was hidden out of sight of the city's inhabitants, to the rear, awaiting his signal to advance. 2: Meanwhile, Joshua himself advanced towards Ai from Jericho with a hand-picked force of 5000, then feigned a retreat in the face of the advancing enemy. 3: Seeing the apparent retreat, the King of Ai ordered his forces out from the city to give chase, leaving it undefended. 4: At Joshua's signal, his hidden force attacked Ai, firing the city. 5: Seeing the flames, the army of Ai turned back, passing Joshua's force, who then attacked. 6: Simultaneously, the other arm of the Israelite force attacked from the other side. Ai and its inhabitants were totally destroyed.

24

Northern Campaign

The Biblical account has presented us thus far with an impression of an overwhelmingly successful military campaign carried out with ruthless despatch by Joshua and the Israelites. When the news of that success in the south reached the north of Canaan, Jabin, King of Hazor, determined to forge a coalition of Canaanite kings to oppose the Israelites. Hazor was one of the most important and powerful of the Canaanite city states and the coalition raised by Jabin was in theory the most powerful the Israelites had to face. The enemy forces were described (*Joshua* 11:4) as '. . . numerous as the sands of the sea, with a huge number of horses and chariots'.

The Canaanite forces chose to deploy their forces for battle at the site of the water supply of the city of Merom, whose king was present for the battle. They needed a plateau such as this to deploy and manoeuvre their chariots effectively.

The account of the battle at Merom is a little confused. The Israelite forces were able to negate the advantage of the Canaanite chariotry:

Yahweh said to Joshua, 'Do not be afraid of them, for by this time tomorrow I shall hand them all over, cut to pieces, to Israel; you will hamstring their horses and burn their chariots.

(*Joshua* 11:6)

Joshua and all the Israelites then fell upon the Canaanites until 'not one

Destruction of Ai, 'The Heap of Ruins', is attributed in the Bible to Joshua and 'all Israel'. Archaeology suggests that the site had been ruined for some centuries prior to the arrival of the Israelites in Canaan.

was left alive'. They hamstrung the enemy horses and burnt the chariots – although this would seem to have been a result, rather than the cause, of victory. Hazor was destroyed:

[all the kings were] put to the sword in compliance with the curse of destruction, as Moses servant of Yahweh, had ordered. Yet of all these towns standing on their mounds, Israel burned none, apart from Hazor, burnt by Joshua

(*Joshua* 11:1)

Once again it is difficult to assess the truth of this account. One problem is that Jabin, King of Hazor, is said to have been killed by Joshua yet is encountered again as king of a rebuilt Hazor in *Judges*, when we are told that he fought against and was destroyed by Deborah and Barak. Certainly Hazor was destroyed at about the time of Joshua's invasion of Canaan but it was a large city with strong defences and it is questionable whether it could have succumbed to the forces of the Israelites, who would seem to have found it impossible to take 'towns on mounds'. Their techniques in siege warfare were very limited at this stage and strongly built positions were too much for them. It may well have been, then, that Hazor was taken by the Sea Peoples, who were moving southwards at the time and had just destroyed the great cities of Alalakh and Ugarit.

Reality of Conquest

It is very difficult in the end to sustain the view propagated by the *Book of Joshua* that the land of Canaan was conquered by a mass invasion of 'All Israel' under Joshua. We are confronted with a picture of a remarkably successful invasion, masterminded by Joshua, who with three campaigns in the centre, the north and the south overwhelms the native Canaanite forces. The ultimate victory of the Israelite forces however is brought about because 'Yahweh, God of Israel, fought for Israel'. The vicious nature of this war against the Canaanites is not disguised.

The text is unambiguous about the consequences for the natives:

All the spoils of the towns, including the livestock, the Israelites took as booty for themselves. But they put all the human beings to the sword until they had destroyed them completely: they did not leave a living soul. What Yahweh had ordered his servant Moses, Moses in turn had ordered Joshua, and Joshua carried it out, leaving nothing undone of what Yahweh had ordered Moses. In consequence, Joshua captured the entire country: the highlands, the whole Negeb and the whole of Goshen, the lowlands, the Arabah, the highlands and the lowlands of Israel.

(*Joshua* 11:14–16)

The invasion of Canaan involved clashes with the Canaanites and in particular brought the Israelites into conflict with the Hupshu, the peasant soldiers of the city states.

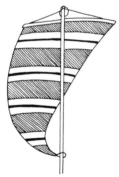

A common sight, frequently depicted in Egyptian paintings and reliefs, were the large sail-like standards, dyed in bright colours. They flew from the battlements of the Canaanite cities besieged and attacked by Joshua's forces.

However, a careful reading of the texts in *Joshua* and *Judges* reveals a much more complex story. The events described in *Joshua* 1–11 communicate the impression of a mass invasion directed towards the conquest of the whole of Canaan, but most occur only in the area later occupied by the tribe of Benjamin. When military operations do take place outside of this limited area it would seem that we are dealing with

26

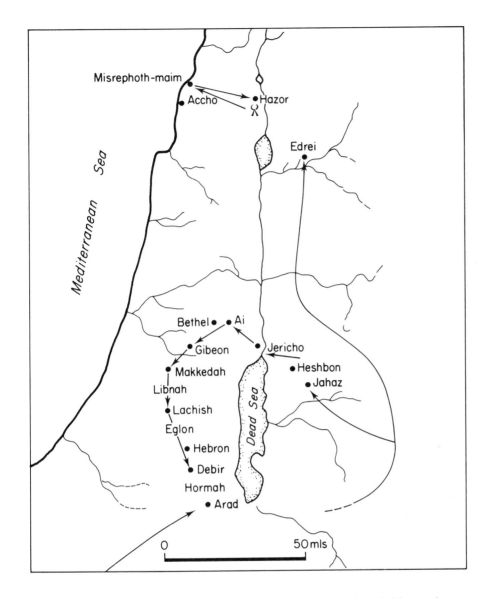

events that took place at a later date which have then either deliberately or as a consequence of confusion been attributed to the time of Joshua. However, even while that account is implying a 'total' conquest it is at the same time revealing that this was far from the case. The text has Yahweh speaking directly to Joshua towards the end of his life.

You are now old and advanced in years, yet there is still a great deal of territory left to be taken possession of . . .

(*Joshua* 13:1–2)

The Archaeological Record

The graphic imagery of the destruction supposedly wrought by the forces of Joshua should in theory find ample testimony in the archaeo-

27

The later Canaanite chariots and their crews were better protected with bronze scale armour. Indeed, those encountered at Mount Gilboa were no doubt crewed by highly trained and well equipped maryannu.

logical record of the period. However, this does not seem to be the case. Certainly the thirteenth century B.C., the period of the Israelite 'invasion,' was a time of widespread destruction of city sites in Canaan west of the River Jordan. Many people have seen in this evidence ample support for the historicity of the Joshua narrative, but there are many reasons for supposing that it was not the Israelites who were responsible for the destruction. In the first place, even where the destruction of sites can be securely dated to this period it is by no means certain that military action was responsible. Furthermore the primary sites whose destruction is described in some detail in the Joshua account of the conquest, such as Jericho and Ai, were not in the thirteenth century B.C. settled on anything like the scale suggested. Certainly, in the case of the 'city' of Ai, the evidence of excavation is that it was already a ruin when the Israelites arrived in Canaan, having been destroyed in about 2350 B.C. Paradoxically, where it is possible to demonstrate evidence of destruction of late Bronze Age Canaanite sites, they all involve cities that are not associated with the Joshua account.

A Different Story?

It was the maryannu *or nobility, who, in return for 'fiefs' of land, gave service to the Canaanite kings of the cities as élite chariot troops.*

In the *Book of Judges* (1:27–36), which is regarded as being a more reliable and authentic account of the settlement than that found in *Joshua*, we find a different picture entirely. It is one of slow infiltration by various groups, with periodic eruptions of fighting between the incoming Israelite settlers. The employment of the phrase 'the Canaanites held their ground' gives us a good insight into the more likely conditions obtaining in Canaan following the 'invasion'. In reality, for the essentially nomadic Israelites entering Canaan, the natives with their superior military organisation and technology were tough nuts to crack. Never-

theless, as the Israelites in their turn became stronger they were able to take on the power of the native Canaanites.

The ultimate absorption of the Canaanite population was a process that itself took many hundreds of years. Thus, a more credible image is that of a limited invasion of the central hill country from east of the Jordan, under the leadership of Joshua, involving the tribes regarded as being of 'The House of Joseph'. Their actual military operations occurred in a small area. The success of these forces may have stimulated Hebrew tribes who had not entered Egypt but had always remained in Canaan to move against the Canaanites with whom they had been living for so long.

Thus, the process of settlement should be seen more in terms of a long-drawn-out process in which individual tribes addressed the situation found in their own areas. In some cases it is not inconceivable that they were supported in their moves against the overlords of the Canaanite cities by other disgruntled and economically alienated non-Israelite groups, who saw in the cause of the Israelites a solution to their own problems. While the evidence is not such as to allow any indisputable conclusion as to the exact nature of the settlement, it was plainly more complex than a cursory reading of the *Book of Joshua* would

Although the capture and destruction of Arad is part of the 'conquest tradition' it is now believed to have been conquered some centuries later. The two sites of the ancient settlement remain clearly visible.

29

suggest. The image of a mass invasion under divine guidance is not one that can be sustained even from the Bible itself. Far from being a mass invasion of 'all Israel' we find the various tribes acting in the early stages more or less independently. It is simply inappropriate to imagine one 'Israelite' nation acting in concert under one leader to realise a collective destiny to take the Promised Land by force of arms.

Judges

For many Biblical scholars, it is only in the *Book of Judges* that one encounters the first realistic picture of the political and social situation in Canaan in the period 1200–1050 B.C., the era before the emergence of the monarchy under Saul in about 1020 B.C.

This was a very turbulent period in Canaan, one in which the overriding political reality was the virtual disappearance of Egyptian authority. Indeed, following the defeat by Ramesses III of the 'Sea Peoples' on the borders of Egypt in about 1186 B.C., Egyptian authority in Canaan virtually ceased. The 'natives' were thereby allowed to attend to their own affairs without interference from the great southern power.

For the Israelite settlers in Canaan, the whole period was one of considerable upheaval marked by the absence of any centralised authority among the tribes. Indeed, the Judges seem to have dealt with problems or threats on the basis of individual or local tribal affiliation,

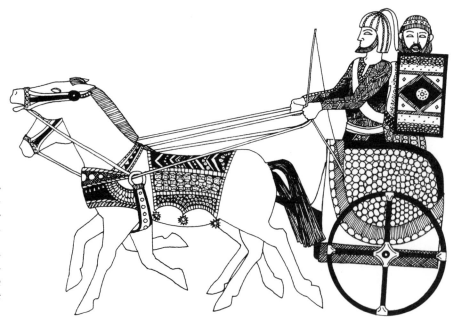

Canaanite chariot from the thirteenth-fourteenth century B.C. showing to good effect the principal weapon in the arsenals of the kings of the city states. It was by burning such chariots and hamstringing the horses that Joshua was able to defeat the Canaanites of the north at the Battle of Merom.

The rulers of the Canaanite city states regularly sent their tribute to the court of the Pharaoh whilst their land was under Egyptian domination.

Devastation of the great city of Hazor occurred at the end of the Bronze Age. Tradition has ascribed its destruction to Joshua, but it is just as possible that the Sea Peoples were responsible. Shown here are the remains of the Pillarred Hall.

with any collective consciousness only appearing later. Significantly, this occurred towards the end of the age of the Judges and was brought about by the overall threat posed by the Philistines to all the tribes of Israel.

Thus, the *Book of Judges* is concerned principally with the conflicts between the Israelites and their Canaanite neighbours in a relatively small geographical area and with the Judges presented as saviours of their tribes or tribal groups.

The stories of the Judges' exploits preserve historical tradition but are structured in a theological manner, organised so that what emerges is called 'The Judges Cycle'. Religious editing of the exploits ensured that the Bible tells of a recurrent pattern in which the Israelites backslide from their commitment to the covenant with Yahweh, by worshipping Canaanite gods. Yahweh then sends oppressors to punish the Israelites, who then call on their God for mercy. Yahweh relents, and from amongst them 'chooses' an individual who is endowed with charisma 'to judge the people'.

Thus, the Judges were not in any way legal officials, but soldiers or local chieftains who saved their people as in the manner of the three we have chosen to concentrate on. Twelve are listed in the Bible, divided as major and minor characters. The exploits of three of the major Judges – Deborah, Gideon and Abimelech – provide a real insight into the conflicts between Israelite and Canaanite in the twelfth century B.C.

Deborah at Mount Tabor

At Mount Tabor, the ill-equipped Israelites, under the charismatic direction of a woman judge, Deborah, brought about the defeat through a clever strategem of a Canaanite chariot force, the very symbol of the military prowess of the city peoples of the plains. Deborah emerges from the account as a fiery leader of her people cast in the same mould as the ancient British Queen Boadicea of the Iceni. Through her inspired leadership a notable victory is realised over the only named Canaanite foe in the *Book of Judges*.

The Biblical account as it stands does – as we should by now have learned to expect – raise problems, not the least being that the enemy is the same Jabin, King of Hazor whose death is reported earlier in the *Book of Joshua*. It seems unlikely we are dealing with two separate kings of the same name, and reasonable therefore to assume that this is an error and to look for an alternative explanation.

We find that alternative source in 'The Song Of Deborah and Barak' in *Judges* 5, one of the oldest pieces of poetry in the Bible. It is a victory song commemorating the triumph of Yahweh over his enemies and praising

Striking swiftly during the 'middle watch', Gideon and his hand-picked force of three hundred destroyed the Midianites and the Amalekites, who for so long had been raiding settlements of their fellow tribesmen.

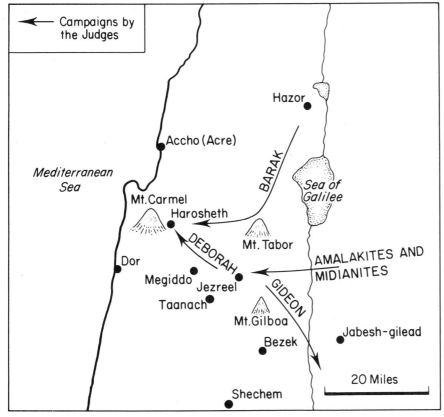

The campaigns of Gideon, Deborah and Abimilech.

the tribes – Machir, Benjamin, Ephraim and Issachar – who responded to the summons of Deborah to fight the foe. Composed (it is thought) shortly after the event, it describes how the Israelites defeated not Jabin but Sisera of Harosheth-ha-Goiim. Indeed, Jabin is not mentioned in the poem at all.

Deborah and Barak

Deborah was a prophetess who dispensed justice from under a palm tree in the hill country of Ephraim. Highly regarded for her wisdom many would come to her for a ruling in the case of disputes believing that in her judgements she was divining the will of Yahweh.

It is not clear why the Canaanites raised an army to attack the Israelites. It may have been as a consequence of Israelite pressure to break the power of the Canaanites, who were separating the northern tribes from those in central Palestine.

It is probable that the Canaanites had raised a large force. It is unrealistic, though, to accept at face value the claim (*Judges* 4:3) that they had 'nine hundred chariots of iron' – it would have been beyond the resources of any Canaanite city to deploy a chariot force of this size. In the fourteenth century B.C. the king of Byblos, a large and powerful city, asking for reinforcements from Egypt, requested only twenty to thirty

Laying siege to the city of Thebez, Abimilech was killed by the woman who threw a millstone at his head. Such an ignominious death was to become, in later times in Israel, a byword for military incompetence.

chariots, implying that this was as large a force as he could effectively employ. In the light of what is known of the small size of the Canaanite city armies, it would seem that even if we subtracted a nought and spoke of ninety chariots we might still be presuming too large a force. Nevertheless, ninety chariots supported by a large feudal levy would have comprised an army likely to have been perceived by the Israelites as huge and, given the fear engendered by the chariots, it is not surprising that the subsequent battle became one in which the defeat of the chariots was enshrined in the folk memory.

The chariots are described as 'of iron', which indicates that we are possibly dealing with 'Sea Peoples' rather than native Canaanites, for it is they who are credited with bringing iron working into Palestine. This would fit quite neatly with the speculation of some scholars that the name Sisera is not Canaanite and that Sisera may have been one of the 'Sea Peoples' who had established themselves on the coastal plain of the Palestinian Shepelah and then expanded into the Plain of Jezreel.

The Battle

The text is unambiguous about where the credit for the outcome of the battle lies. It is Deborah who had to cajole a seemingly reluctant Barak to take the field against Sisera. And the strategy, too, was Deborah's. It was based on an intimate knowledge of the terrain. Clearly the Israelites would stand no chance if they opposed the enemy on the plain, where their chariots could be used with devastating effect against the poorly equipped Israelite tribal levy armed only with spears, bows and swords. Somehow Sisera would have to be enticed on to ground where the power of his chariots could be negated.

Sisera was stationed with his army at Harosheth-ha-Goiim in the lee of Mount Carmel, but when he heard that Deborah and Barak had deployed their forces on Mount Tabor he decided to move, seeing in the Israelite disposition a threat to his line of communications with the north. As Deborah had foreseen, the Canaanite force advanced towards Tabor following the banks of the River Kishon. The Vale of Esdraelon

through which they advanced was a wide and fertile valley bounded to the north by the Hills of Galilee and to the south by Mount Gilboa and Mount Carmel. Along the southeastern edge of the vale flowed the River Kishon, normally a small stream flowing through an almost dry riverbed. However short, intense rainstorms transformed the river very quickly into a raging torrent and turned the deep rich soil of the vale into a glutinous morass inimicable to man, beast and chariot alike. Deborah's plan was dependent upon the elements playing their part and when the Canaanite army with the chariots in the van swung into view there must have been many anxious Israelite eyes looking skywards for the clouds that were to be the harbingers of their salvation and of the destruction of the Canaanites.

To the unsophisticated Israelites, the sight of Sisera's forces must have caused much fear and agitation and perhaps not a little silent questioning as to the wisdom of taking on such a formidable foe. As the sun glinted off the Canaanite shields and spearpoints and shimmered on the bronze scale armour of the charioteers doubt must have crept into the Israelites' hearts. Here below them, in all their martial glory, were the mighty chariots of the warlords of the plains. But as the sky darkened and the rain began to fall, the ground began to soften and the advancing chariots ground slowly to a halt as their wheels bogged down in the mud.

The 'Song of Deborah' paints a vivid picture of the Israelite soldiery pouring down the slopes of Mount Tabor and gaining a remarkable victory over the feared Canaanite chariots. As can be seen, the steep incline would produce considerable impetus in any descending forces.

35

The rain fell harder, turning the ground into a morass. Slithering and sliding horses, whipped relentlessly by their drivers, stumbled and fell. Above the sound of panicking men, the barked commands of the officers and the whinnying of the horses another noise could be heard – an immense roar as the rain on the mountain came pouring down into the riverbed, carrying all before it and overflowing the banks. As the Canaanites struggled to save themselves from the waters, Deborah turned to Barak, yelling with eyes ablaze:

Up! For today is the day when Yahweh has put Sisera into your power. Is Yahweh not marching at your head?

With only a slight hesitation and after one final scan of the mounting chaos in the valley below, Barak raised his sword and thrust it forward to signal the advance. Screaming a battlecry that could be heard even above the roar of the torrent, the crash of the thunder and the hammering of the rain, the Israelites scrambled down from the mountain and threw themselves into the wild mêlée of the now totally disorganised Canaanite troops. Jumping onto the chariots they dragged down the drivers and the mail-coated archers, their swords executing fearful carnage in the mud. Men and horses were ruthlessly despatched as the Israelites sought to exorcise with their blades the legacy of the hate and fear engendered over many years by the Canaanite chariots.

Song of Victory

Somehow Sisera was able to save himself from the slaughter, but as the 'Song of Barak' records with grim satisfaction he had not long to live. Some hours later, on foot and fleeing for his life, he came, exhausted and hungry, to a tent and presented himself to the woman within. The welcome he received gave no hint of the fate that awaited him:

> Most blessed of women be Jael
> (the wife of Heber the Kenite);
> of tent dwelling women, may she be most blessed!
>
> He asked her for water; she gave him milk;
> she offered him curds in a lordly dish.
> She reached her hand out to seize the peg,
> her right hand to seize the workman's mallet.
>
> She hammered Sisera, she crushed his head,
> she pierced his temple and shattered it.
> Between her feet, he crumpled, he fell.
> Where hè crumpled, there he fell, destroyed.
>
> (Judges 5:25–27)

The last few verses of 'The Song of Deborah and Barak' celebrate the great victory of Mount Tabor as a victory of the God of the Israelites over his enemies. The ultimate consequence of Yahweh's saving act in the battle against Sisera was that 'the country had peace for forty years'.

36

Gideon and the Midianites

The Israelites did what was evil in Yahweh's eyes, and for seven years Yahweh handed them over to Midian; and Midian bore down heavily on Israel.

(*Judges* 6:1–2)

Expressed in political rather than religious terms this means that the Midianites had established supremacy over the Israelites. That these nomadic raiders were able for so long to hold some of the Israelite tribes in thrall tells us much about conditions prevailing in Canaan at this time. The battle against Sisera had taken place in the western end of the Jezreel valley, but Gideon's exploits occurred in the eastern part of the valley. Clearly Egyptian influence and power in this part of Canaan had disappeared and the ease with which the nomadic Midianites were able to move into the area and terrorise and raid the Israelite settlements suggests that even the power of the Canaanite cities was in eclipse. It was also the lack of any central political authority amongst the Israelites that allowed the Midianites to inflict so much havoc on them and the distress they caused was great:

Whenever Israel sowed seed the Midianites would march up with Amalek and the sons of the east. They would march on Israel. They would pitch camp on their territory and destroy the produce of the country as far as Gaza. They left Israel nothing to live on, not a sheep or an ox or a donkey, for they came up as thick as locusts with their camels and their tents; they and their camels were innumerable, they invaded the country to pillage it.

(*Judges* 6:34–35)

The story of Gideon's defeat of the Midianites gives us a remarkable insight into the way in which the Israelites of the time fought a campaign and worked out their strategy. We can identify three distinct phases in the campaign. We have the recruitment of the forces, the preparation for battle and the planning of the campaign.

The Midianites and their allies, the Amalekites, encamped in the Jezreel valley with all their families, animals and other possessions. This provided Gideon with the opportunity he had been waiting for. Always before the Midianites had launched raids against the Israelite settlements in true nomadic fashion. They adopted hit and run tactics, utilising the speed of their camels to exploit the element of surprise and to extricate themselves from difficult situations. Because of this, the infantry forces of the Israelite tribal levy had been unable to come to grips with them. By bringing their whole settlement with them the Midianites had rendered themselves far more vulnerable to attack. It was their inability to move quickly, hampered as they were by the presence of their flocks and families, that Gideon intended to exploit. Having received the news that the enemy had encamped he sent word to call out the levy:

He sounded the horn and Abiezer rallied behind him. He sent messengers throughout

The Book of Judges *tells how the Israelites were seduced into worshipping Canaanite gods such as Baal. Consequently, Yahweh raised up enemies to oppress and punish them.*

Manasseh, and Manasseh too rallied behind him; he sent messengers to Asher, Zebulun and Naphtali, and they marched out to meet him.

(Judges 6:34–35)

The summons produced a force far larger than was needed by Gideon. His plan depended more on stealth and surprise than on fielding a large militia army. From the 32,000 men who responded to his call he selected 10,000 and from these he carefully chose just three hundred. His method of selecting these three hundred is deserving of some explanation, for on first reading it appears a strange way to select warriors:

So Gideon took the people down to the waterside, and Yahweh said to him, 'All those who lap the water with their tongues, as a dog laps, put on one side. And all those who kneel down to drink, put these on the other side. The number of those who lapped with their hands to their mouth was three hundred; all the rest of the people knelt to drink. Yahweh then said to Gideon, 'With the three hundred who lapped the water I shall rescue you and put Midian into your power. Let the people as a whole disperse to their homes.' So they took the people's provisions and their horns, and then Gideon sent all the Israelites back to their tents, keeping only the three hundred. The camp of Midian was below his in the valley.

(Judges 7:5–8)

Gideon may perhaps have chosen those who lay down to drink because they showed care to present the enemy with a reduced target as well as a willingness to tolerate the discomfort caused thereby. Such skill and hardiness was essential to his plan to destroy the enemy encampment.

Then he ordered the men of Naphtali, Asher and Manasseh to move against the water holes between the Midianites' encampment and the line of retreat that they would be forced to take in the aftermath of the attack. The task of these men would be to destroy the fleeing enemy in detail.

That night Gideon and his servant stole into the Midianite camp and overheard a conversation between two guards which revealed their low morale. After a final scout around the camp all was ready.

The Attack

Gideon had divided up his men into three groups of a hundred. He issued each man with a horn and an empty pitcher into which was placed a torch so that the light was concealed. Then he told them:

Watch me, and do as I do. When I reach the edge of the camp whatever I do, you must do also. I shall blow my horn, and so will all those who are with me; you too will then blow your horns all around the camp and shout, 'For Yahweh and for Gideon!'

(Judges 7:17–18)

Assigning each group to one side of the encampment – north, west and south – but leaving the east open so that the Midianites could escape towards the Jordan, Gideon ordered his forces down into the valley. As surprise was of the essence he took care to arrive at the edge of the Midianite camp at the dead of night. It was at the time of the middle watch, just after the guards had been changed; the new guards were not yet fully awake and their eyes were still unaccustomed to the darkness. Gideon stood up and his signal shout shattered the silence of the night: 'the sword for Yahweh and for Gideon!'

As if with one voice, his men took up the battle cry. Gideon took his clay pitcher, smashed it with his blade, and threw it at the nearest tent. He cut down the surprised guard. His men followed his example and poured into the camp. Flames leapt up as torches caught the tents alight. Panic-stricken Midianites scrambled into the night, stumbling and falling, their minds clouded by sleep. Babies cried and screamed as they clung to their mothers' breasts. The Israelites pushed into the camp, scything down the Midianites and shooting them with arrows as they emerged from their tents. They spared neither man, woman nor child. Amid the confusion Midianite killed Midianite in the half-light of the dancing flames. Gideon's men began to herd the enemy towards the eastern end of the camp. Acrid smoke from the burning tents drifted across the camp, and in the terror that developed many Midianites were crushed to death as they tried to escape the blades of the Israelites. Others disappeared, trampled beneath the feet of the snorting and grunting camels as, maddened by the heat, they blundered hither and thither. With their bronze khopeshes and iron swords, the three hundred slashed their way forward, inexorably pressing the surviving Midianites eastwards and out of the camp. The dead and dying were left behind amid a conflagration that was becoming one great funeral pyre.

With the survivors of the Midianite encampment in full flight in the direction of the Jordan, Gideon set off in hot pursuit, his intention being to finish the Midianite threat once and for all. After crossing the Jordan he finally ran to ground the Midianite kings, Zebah and Zalmunna, and killed them.

The men of Succoth, we are told, were unwilling to help Gideon and his men in their pursuit of the enemy. This suggests that they were not at that stage prepared to risk the vengeance of the Midianites should Gideon fail. Indeed, they demanded evidence that the Midianite kings were dead before they would give supplies to the Israelites:

Are the hands of Zebah and Zalmunna already in your grasp that we should give bread to your army?

(*Judges* 8:6)

The request was literally to be shown the hands of the dead kings. The presentation of some part of the body as evidence of death was a common procedure used all over the ancient Near East. In the time of David foreskins were often taken, but where this was not possible because the enemy was circumcised (as it seems the Midianites were) a hand would be taken instead. This was also a common Egyptian practice. The Assyrians had a penchant for cutting off the heads of the dead so that the scribes could count the enemy slain for the record in the royal annals.

The main hand weapon of Joshua's soldiers, as of all armies in the ancient Near East at this time, was the bronze bladed khopesh, a curved sword for slashing.

Gideon's campaign was the outcome of careful planning, rapid execution taking advantage of knowledge of the local terrain and a ruthless follow-up. His reward was to be offered the crown by his people:

> The men of Israel said to Gideon, 'Rule over us, you and your son and your grandson, since you have rescued us from power of Midian.
>
> (*Judges* 8:22)

He rejected their offer, on the grounds that 'Yahweh shall rule you', but his 'son' Abimelech was not averse to assuming a royal mantle for himself. His story is a strange yet revealing and significant one.

Abimelech 'The King'

The story of the rise and fall of Abimelech in the *Book of Judges* stands apart from the other accounts concerning those 'called' by Yahweh to save 'his' people. He was *not* called – and strictly speaking he was not even an Israelite.

Thus, his inclusion within the *Book of Judges* may well have served to make a theological point with respect to political power and kingship: in Israel no man could be King unless Yahweh designated him such. The rise and fall of this ruthless individual also gives us a good insight into the reality of relations between the Israelites and their Canaanite neighbours and the degree to which for the greater part of the time following their arrival in Canaan most of the tribes managed to forge some kind of accommodation with the natives and to live in peace with them. They did not live in a state of perpetual warfare.

Offer of Strength

Tradition has Abimelech as the 'son' of Gideon, and he is called in the Biblical text the 'son of Jerrubbaal', which is an alternative title for Gideon; but there is good reason to believe, that there was no relationship between them.

> Gideon had seventy sons begotten by him, for he had many wives. His concubine who lived at Shechem, also bore him a son, to whom he gave the name Abimelech.
>
> (*Judges* 8:31–32)

What this probably implies is that some kind of special relationship existed between the tribe of Manasseh and the people of the city of Shechem. This relationship allowed for intermarriage between the Canaanites and their Israelite neighbours, an occurrence unlikely at a later date. It has been suggested that, far from being an ordinary Shechemite woman, Abimelech's mother was the daughter of one of the ruling Canaanite aristocracy of the city, which would account for his seemingly easy acceptance by the Shechemites as their ruler. Dominating the tribe of Manasseh and thus Shechem also at this time was the clan of Jerrubbaal. The power that the Israelites had over them was not to the liking of the ruling class at Shechem but, until Abimelech presented himself to them with an offer to help reassert Shechemite dominance in the area, albeit on his terms, they could do little about it. What Abimelech offered them may not have been to their liking but it was infinitely preferable to domination by the Israelites. What emerges plainly is the Machiavellian nature of Abimelech, who is prepared to exploit this antipathy for his own ambitious ends. Consider the proposal he puts to the rulers of the city:

Abimelech son of Jerubbaal confronted his mother's brothers at Shechem and to them and to the whole clan of his maternal grandfather's family, he said, 'Please put this question to the leading men of Shechem: Which is better for you: to be ruled by seventy people – all Jerrubbaal's sons – or to be ruled by one? Remember too I am your flesh and bone.' His mother's brothers said all this on his behalf to all the leading men of Shechem, and their feelings swayed them to follow Abimelech, since they argued, 'He is our brother'.

When his offer had been accepted Abimelech expected the Shechemites to provide him with the means of procuring the services of soldiers to destroy 'the sons of Jerubbaal.' Entering the temple to Baal-Berith the Shechemites took from the treasury 70 shekels of silver. With this sum Abimelech proceeded to recruit a body of mercenaries who would view him, as their paymaster, as their leader. That such men were available for hiring suggests that conditions in Canaan may well have been much the same in the eleventh and twelfth centuries as they had been at the time of the Amarna letters, when small wars between the city states were fought using mercenary forces hired from amongst the Hapiru. With this mercenary force Abimelech moved rapidly against the Jerubbaal's clan city of Ophrah and there killed all the 'sons of Jerubbaal' save one who managed to escape.

Rule of the Sword

In reward for his action the aristocracy of the city made Abimelech their King, although it began to emerge quite quickly that he aspired to greater things. He may have been spurred on not only by ambition but also by his recognition that in the final analysis his power was at the mercy of his hired mercenaries. Their personal loyalty to him was dubious and in direct proportion to his willingness to reward them. Thus the process of expanding his domain to encompass the rule of the Manassite and Ephraimite clans in the mountains around Shechem was the inevitable consequence of the nature of his rule.

To the Shechemites the revelation that Abimelech was little more than an adventurer intent on carving out a kingdom for himself at their expense led to the emergence of an opposition to his rule. Their grievances were further compounded when Abimelech moved his ruling seat from Shechem to Arumah in Ephraimite territory and installed in

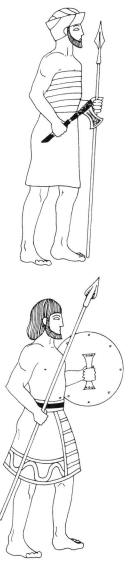

Probable appearance of Hapiru in the thirteenth century B.C. It was the availability of freebooters such as these that allowed Abimelech to raise his own 'private' army.

Shechem an official to govern the city in his name. Deciding that Abimelech could no longer be trusted, the Shechemites charged Abimelech with disloyalty and gathered a force to challenge him. Moving quickly, Abimelech brought his mercenary forces to Shechem and attacked it.

Battle of Shechem

The description of Abimelech's taking of the city gives us a good insight into the techniques employed in the twelfth and eleventh centuries B.C for the reduction of fortified settlements:

All that day Abimilech attacked the town. He stormed it and slaughtered the people inside, razed the town and sowed it with salt.

The attack of Shechem opens with a battle outside the walls of the city, with Abimelech's mercenary troops attacking in three units – the standard procedure of the time for the deployment of troops for battle. Two units hid in the fields, waiting for the Shechemites to deploy their forces in front of the city walls. These units were dispatched to pin down and destroy the enemy while he with the remaining troops under his command headed to the city to prevent the gates being closed and to gain a quick access to the city itself. The Shechemite forces were caught by surprise and destroyed in detail as they attempted to deploy into line, one of the moments of maximum vulnerability for any army. Abimelech's forces then broke in to the city itself, having taken the city gate, the point of greatest weakness in the outer wall defences. Those of the citizens who had managed to escape the blades of Abimelech's mercenaries, some one thousand in all, made their way to the inner citadel of the city, which was also the temple of the god Baal-Berith.

Archaeological excavations of the site of Shechem, identified with Tell Balatah to the east of the modern town of Nablus, have revealed a building some 69 feet by 86 feet which is thought to be the house of Baal-Berith. Like other Canaanite temples, the House of Baal was built in the form of a fortified tower. Such buildings are depicted on Egyptian wall reliefs of Ramesses II in the Ramesseum and show a formidable defensive structure with crenellated walls on four sides allowing the defenders to rain down stones, spears and arrows on any attackers crossing the open ground around the tower.

The problem of taking a building like this was solved by Abimelech:

He went up Mount Zalmon with all his men. Then taking an axe in his hands, he cut off the branch of a tree and put it on his shoulder, and said to the men with him, 'Hurry and do what you have seen me do.' Each of his men similarly cut off a branch; then following Abimelech, they piled all the branches

(*Judges* 9:48–49)

Then, under cover of their shields, they piled the branches against the

42

gate of the citadel and set fire to this huge bonfire, burning to death all of those inside.

There could be no doubting now that there existed no warrant or legitimacy for Abimelech's rule except through the sword. The very nature of his power thus required a continual resort to force to maintain his position and it was in the act of attacking another city that he met his death, in a manner so demeaning that it became a byword for military incompetence in Israel.

Death in Dishonour
The death of Abimelech occurred in circumstances almost identical to those at Shechem. In this case the town under siege was Thebez, possibly

Based upon a relief from Karnak (now believed to date from the time of Merneptah's campaign in Canaan) this fortified city must have typified major settlements throughout Canaan into the time of the Judges.

This version of the recurring theme of a Pharaoh 'smiting the Asiatic' is set in Canaan showing the type of central tower under whose walls Abimelech met his death.

the same settlement as that on the border of Neapolis mentioned by the Roman writer Eusebius.

In the middle of the town there was a fortified tower in which all the men of the town took refuge. They locked the door behind them and climbed to the roof of the tower and attacked it. As he was approaching the door of the tower to set it on fire, a woman threw down a millstone on his head and cracked his skull.

(*Judges* 9:50–53)

But Abimelech had no taste for dying an ignominious death, by the hand of a woman. He appealed to his armour bearer:

Draw your sword and kill me, so that it will not be said of me that 'A woman killed him'. His armour bearer ran him through, and he died. When the men of Israel saw that Abimelech was dead, they dispersed to their homes.

(*Judges* 9:54–55)

Alas, he could not escape the verdict of posterity. In 2 *Samuel*, we find Joab, David's army commander, sending word back to the King and offering the death of Abimelech as an awful example of military ineptitude:

Why did you go near the town to give battle? Didn't you know that they would shoot from the ramparts? Who killed Abimelech, son of Jerubbaal? Wasn't it a woman who dropped a millstone from the ramparts, causing his death at Thebez?

(2 *Samuel* 11:20–21)

44

With Abimelech's death the arrangement between Shechem and Man-asseh returned to what it had been before his attempt to carve out for himself a kingdom. He left behind no lasting achievement and, while he was the first man in Israel to be called a king, in no way did his example influence the emergence of the Kingship in Israel under Saul. His place then in the *Book of Judges* is hard to understand, for far from being a saviour of his people he was nothing more than a military adventurer.

The Ultimate Enemy

The struggle and conflicts continued. Yet one recurring theme began to be dominant in the warring and fighting. Of all the enemies faced by the Hebrew tribes in the time of the Judges, none could match the efficiency, vigour and ruthlessness of the Philistines.

Having been settled in the coastlands of the Palestinian Shephelah by Ramesses III, following their abortive attempt to invade Egypt in 1186 B.C., these highly organised groups of the 'Sea Peoples' posed a threat of a profound nature to the very existence of the tribes of Israel.

It was out of the Philistine threat to Israel that the nascent movement to a more effective and centralised political structure began to evolve. In time, it was the Philistine menace, moving inland from the coast into the Hebrew heartland, that was to see the emergence of the monarchy under Saul and David. It was a process that was to transform the tribes of Israel into a nation.

Recoiling from the defeat inflicted on them on the border of Egypt by Ramesses III in 1186 B.C., the Sea Peoples settled in Canaan. Based upon the Hedinet-habu relief, this depiction of a group of Sea People as prisoners includes (second figure on the right) a Philistine. Of all the enemies of Israel, they posed the greatest threat to their existence. Their predatory attacks on the lands of the Hebrew settlement provided the catalyst for the emergence of the monarchy under Saul and David.

The Stela of Merneptah

Placing any accurate date on Joshua's invasion of Canaan with the tribes that comprised 'The House of Joseph' is difficult. There is only one source extant prior to the ninth century B.C. that mentions 'Israel' by name. This is the famous granite 'Israel Stela' of the Pharaoh Merneptah, which purports to record his victories in Canaan early in his reign.

There is general agreement that the stela itself was inscribed in the fifth year of the Pharaoh's reign. But there is no consensus as to the year of his succession, suggested dates ranging from 1238 B.C. to about 1213 B.C. The consensus is that the stela makes reference to an Egyptian punitive campaign by Merneptah (or his son) in Canaan, after the death of his father Ramesses II, sometime in the last three decades of the thirteenth century B.C.

From the names on the stela it is possible to see that after following the route of the coastal route, the Egyptian forces moved, in turn, against the cities of Ashkelon and Gezer. They then moved inland into the hill country. There, to the south of Yenoam, which was also named, the army of the Pharaoh came to grips with the forces of 'Israel'. The stela text is written in hymnic form:

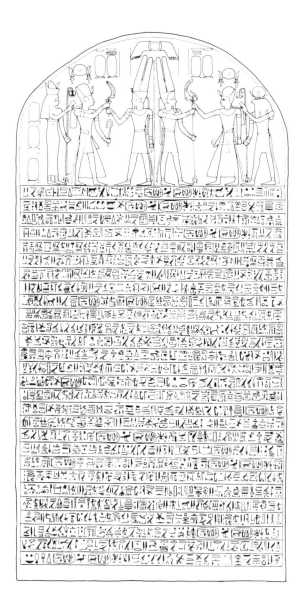

> *Plundered is Canaan with every evil;*
> *Carried off is Ashkelon; seized upon is Gezer;*
> *Yanoam is made as that which does not exist;*
> *Israel is laid waste, his seed is not;*
> *Hurru is become a widow for Egypt!*
> *All lands together they are pacified;*
> *Everyone who is restless, he has been bound.*

Of greatest significance is that 'Israel' is preceded by a hieroglyphic sign used to designate 'a people' – indicating the presence of a wandering or tribal group. Of course, Joshua and his invading tribes were fighting against the Canaanites. But the Egyptians, if indeed they did encounter them, were not likely to have made much distinction between warring groups among the general dissident activity that the expedition had been sent to suppress.

The Bible gives no hint of any encounter between the Israelites and the army of the Pharaoh and some scholars see no significance in this 'encounter' of Egypt with 'Israel', suggesting that the tribes involved were those who had been settled in Canaan for many centuries. But it seems much more reasonable to infer that the Egyptians *did* come into contact with a group of nomadic tribes collectively known as 'Israel' – the very people being led by Joshua.

Chronology of Events

Whilst it is not possible to give dates in such a chronology with any real certainty, the following represents a feasible and realistic time scale of the main events. However, it has to be noted that some sources place the Joseph narratives much later.

1900–1700 B.C.	Likely period of the Patriarchs.
1720–1580 B.C.	Rule of the Hyksos in Egypt.
1580–1567 B.C.	Possible time of Joseph in Egypt.
1560–1200 B.C.	Canaan under domination of Egypt.
1270–1260 B.C.	Likely time of the Exodus.
1230–1207 B.C.	Merneptah Stela; evidence of Israel in Egypt.
1210–1190 B.C.	Probable 'invasion' of Canaan by 'House of Joseph' under Joshua.
1186 B.C.	Ramesses III defeats 'Sea Peoples' on Egypt's borders; Philistines begin settlement of Palestinian coastal plain.
1150–1050 B.C.	Probable period of the Judges.

Bibliography

Aldred, C. *The Egyptians* Thames and Hudson, 1987.

Anderson, B. *The Living World of the Old Testament*, Longman, 1976.

Bright, J.A. *History of Israel*, 3rd Edition, Philadelphia, 1981.

Edwards, I.E.S. (ed) *Cambridge Ancient History*, Vol. 1 (part 2B) Vol. 2 (parts 1 and 2A), Cambridge University Press, 1971, 1973 and 1975.

Ferrill, A. *The Origins of War* Thames and Hudson, 1986.

Finegan, J. *Archaeological History of the Ancient Middle East*, Dorset, 1979.

Grant, M. *The History of Ancient Israel*, Weidenfeld & Nicolson, 1984.

Jagersma, H.A. *History of Israel in the Old Testament Period* SCM, 1982.

Kitchen, K.A. *Pharaoh Triumphant* Aris and Phillips, 1982.

Miller, M.J. and Hayes, J.H. *A History of Ancient Israel and Judah* SCM, 1986.

Negev, A (ed) *The Archaeological Encyclopedia of the Holy Land* Nelson, 1986.

Noth, M. *The History of Israel* SCM, 1958.

Pritchard, J. *The Ancient Near East*, Vols 1 and 2, Princeton, 1958 and 1975.

Pritchard, J. (ed) *The Times Atlas of the Bible* Times Books, 1987.

Sandars, N.K. *The Sea Peoples* Thames and Hudson, 1978.

Stillman, N. & Tallis, N. *Armies of the Ancient Near East* Wargames Research Group, 1984.

Time-Life Books *The Israelites* Time Life Books, 1975.

Yadin, Y. *The Art of Warfare in Biblical Lands* International Publishing Co., 1963.

Illustrations

Colour plates by Richard Hook
Line illustrations by Suzie Hole
Maps and diagrams by Chartwell Illustrators
Photographs and other illustrations courtesy of: British Museum (pages 11, 12, 14, 15, 19, 20 and 31); Zev Radovan (pages 23, 25, 29, 31 and 35)

Index

Page numbers in *italics* refer to illustrations